STARS

Isaac Asimov

Illustrated by Herb Herrick · Diagrams by Mike Gordon

FOLLETT PUBLISHING COMPANY Chicago

Library of Congress Catalog Card Number: 68-13033   Second Printing

ISBN 0 695-48329-3 Titan binding ISBN 0 695-88329-1 Trade binding

The Sun is a star. On its surface the temperature is about 10,000° F.

A star is a giant ball of gas, so hot that it glows very brightly. The nearest star to us is our Sun. It is about 93 million miles away.

Even though it is very far away, we can see the Sun as a ball of light. That is because the Sun is so large. If we traveled away from the Sun in a space ship, the Sun would seem to get smaller. If we went out far enough, our Sun would be too far away to see as a ball of light. It would look like a glowing dot.

The light of the stars comes to us as a narrow beam. Moving air makes this beam of light bend a bit. The star seems to move a little and we say the star is twinkling.

We see many such dots of light in the sky on a clear night. These are the stars. If the night is really dark, we may be able to see more than 2,000 of them at one time. Each star would look something like the Sun if only it were much closer.

Faint stars, hidden by Earth's
air from people on the ground,
can be seen from airless space.

Stars shine during the daytime, too. But
when the Sun rises, its bright light floods the
Earth. Some of the Sun's light is scattered by
the air, making the daytime sky seem blue.

In space, where there is no air, the sky is
always black and the stars do not twinkle. A
man in space can see far more stars than a man
on Earth.

The brighter stars make groups in the sky called CONSTELLATIONS. Long ago, people thought the star groups looked like men, or animals, or things. The people of long ago gave names to the constellations. Today's sky scientists, or astronomers, still use the old names.

The Big Dipper is a star pattern that is easy to find. It is part of the constellation Ursa Major, or the Greater Bear. Near by is Ursa Minor, the Smaller Bear.

The dippers are easy to find in the northern sky. You may find them tilted different ways.

URSA MAJOR — URR-sah MAY-jer
URSA MINOR — URR-sah MY-ner

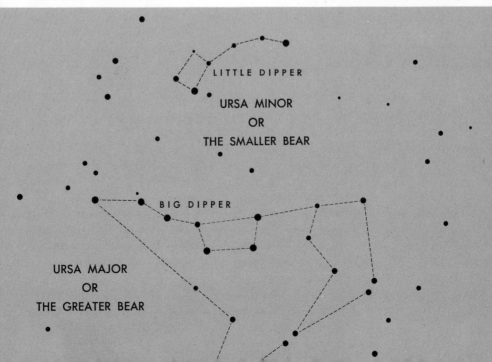

LITTLE DIPPER

URSA MINOR
OR
THE SMALLER BEAR

BIG DIPPER

URSA MAJOR
OR
THE GREATER BEAR

The constellation Orion is one of the most beautiful. The Greeks of long ago thought this star group looked like a giant hunter with club, shield, and a belt with a sword hanging down.

The brighter stars in the sky have names. Some were given by the Greeks and Romans, and some by the Arabs, who were the greatest astronomers a thousand years ago.

We see Orion in the winter sky when we look southward.

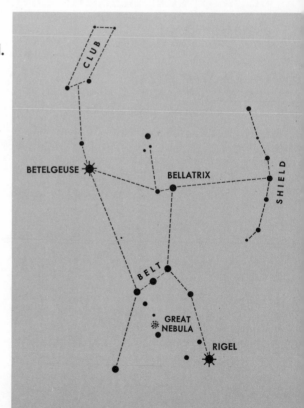

MAGNITUDE OF STARS

* First Magnitude
● Second Magnitude
● Third Magnitude
● Fourth Magnitude
· Fifth Magnitude

ORION — uh-RY-un
BETELGEUSE — BAY-tel-juice
BELLATRIX — BELL-uh-tricks
RIGEL — RY-jel

8

The names of the constellations come down to us from the Roman people of long ago, who spoke Latin. Astronomers still use the Latin names. Near Orion is a group of stars that people thought looked like a dog. It is called the Greater Dog (in Latin, Canis Major). Near it is the Smaller Dog, Canis Minor.

The Greater Dog has the brightest star in all the sky, Sirius the Dog Star. The Smaller Dog also has a bright star, Procyon.

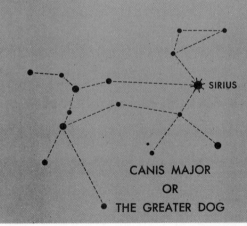

CANIS MINOR
OR
THE SMALLER DOG

PROCYON

SIRIUS

CANIS MAJOR
OR
THE GREATER DOG

CANIS MAJOR — KAY-nis MAY-jer
CANIS MINOR — KAY-nis MY-ner
SIRIUS — SEAR-ee-us
PROCYON — PRO-sy-un

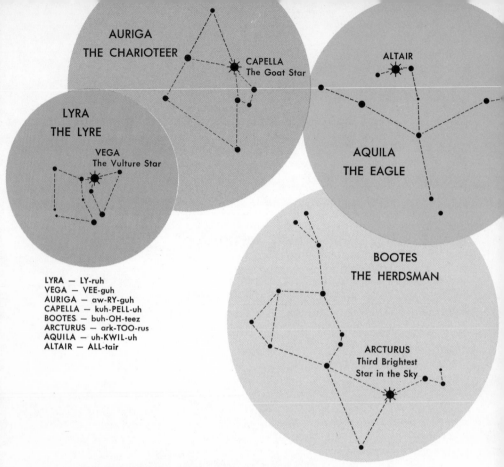

AURIGA
THE CHARIOTEER

CAPELLA
The Goat Star

ALTAIR

LYRA
THE LYRE

VEGA
The Vulture Star

AQUILA
THE EAGLE

LYRA — LY-ruh
VEGA — VEE-guh
AURIGA — aw-RY-guh
CAPELLA — kuh-PELL-uh
BOOTES — buh-OH-teez
ARCTURUS — ark-TOO-rus
AQUILA — uh-KWIL-uh
ALTAIR — ALL-tair

BOOTES
THE HERDSMAN

ARCTURUS
Third Brightest
Star in the Sky

The twenty brightest stars in the sky are called FIRST MAGNITUDE stars. Stars that are a little fainter are called second magnitude stars, and so on. The dimmest stars we can see with our eyes alone are about sixth magnitude.

The picture shows some famous star groups that have first magnitude stars.

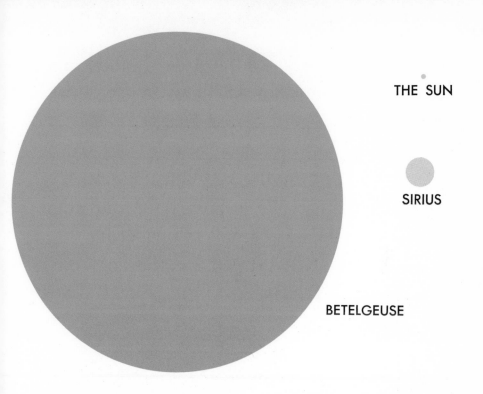

THE SUN

SIRIUS

BETELGEUSE

Some stars seem bright because they are near us. Sirius, the brightest star we see, is not too far away compared to other stars. Some stars seem to be bright because they are very large. Betelgeuse in the constellation Orion is 30 times as far away as Sirius. But it seems bright because it is about 500 times as large as our Sun.

If you were to watch the stars all night long, you would see that they don't stay in one place. They all seem to move across the sky.

The stars seem to move because the Earth turns around and around, or rotates. We don't feel the Earth turn. We seem to stand still while the sky turns. Our sky seems to turn about a place called the NORTH POLE of the sky.

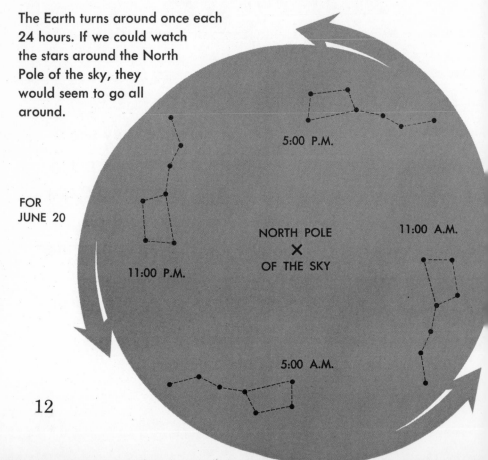

The Earth turns around once each 24 hours. If we could watch the stars around the North Pole of the sky, they would seem to go all around.

5:00 P.M.

FOR
JUNE 20

NORTH POLE
X
OF THE SKY

11:00 A.M.

11:00 P.M.

5:00 A.M.

The North Pole of the sky is very near the last star of the Little Dipper's handle. This star is called the Pole Star, or Polaris. All the stars in our sky seem to turn around Polaris, which does not seem to move much. It stays always in the north, so it is called the North Star. People without compasses have used Polaris to find directions at night.

The two stars at the front of the Big Dipper's bowl mark out a line that points to Polaris. These stars are called the Pointers. Polaris is quite bright, of the second magnitude. If you can find the Big Dipper, you should be able to find the North Star.

LITTLE DIPPER

POLARIS

BIG DIPPER

POLARIS — poh-LAIR-iss

POINTER

POINTER

13

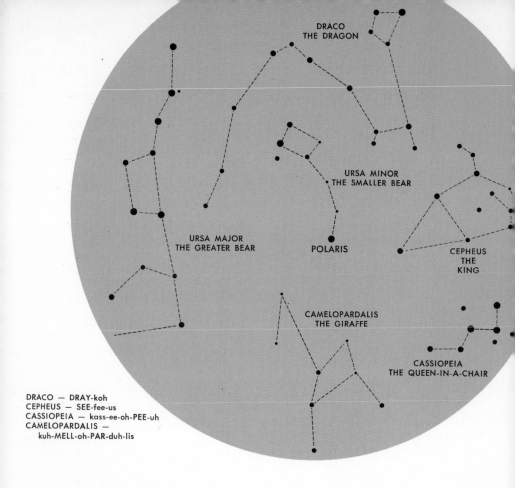

DRACO
THE DRAGON

URSA MINOR
• THE SMALLER BEAR

URSA MAJOR
THE GREATER BEAR

POLARIS

CEPHEUS
THE
KING

CAMELOPARDALIS
THE GIRAFFE

CASSIOPEIA
THE QUEEN-IN-A-CHAIR

DRACO — DRAY-koh
CEPHEUS — SEE-fee-us
CASSIOPEIA — kass-ee-oh-PEE-uh
CAMELOPARDALIS —
   kuh-MELL-oh-PAR-duh-lis

People in North America, northern Europe, and northern Asia see the Pole Star high in the sky. Some constellations near it never go beneath the HORIZON, or place where the sky seems to meet the ground. This picture shows constellations around the North Pole of the sky.

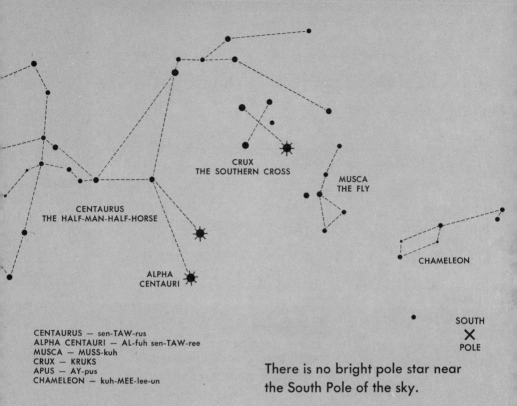

CRUX
THE SOUTHERN CROSS

MUSCA
THE FLY

CENTAURUS
THE HALF-MAN-HALF-HORSE

CHAMELEON

ALPHA
CENTAURI

SOUTH
X
POLE

CENTAURUS — sen-TAW-rus
ALPHA CENTAURI — AL-fuh sen-TAW-ree
MUSCA — MUSS-kuh
CRUX — KRUKS
APUS — AY-pus
CHAMELEON — kuh-MEE-lee-un

There is no bright pole star near
the South Pole of the sky.

The South Pole of the sky is opposite the
North Pole. It cannot be seen from North
America or Europe. It is always below the
horizon, and so are the stars near it.

People in South America, Africa, southern
Asia, and Australia see the constellations in
the picture. Centaurus has a bright star that
is our Sun's nearest star neighbor.

15

If we stand looking south, we see that some stars seem to rise in the east and set in the west. This happens to all constellations except those very near the North Pole of the sky.

As the Earth rotates, we are carried out of the night side of the sky with all its stars we can see, and into the day side. We cannot see the stars in the half of the sky that is lit by sunlight.

If we watched the south all night, the constellatic would move across it fro to west.

EAST

The Earth rotates once each day. But it also travels around the Sun once each year. Because of this, the sky picture changes a little each night. The constellations rise in the east a little earlier than they did the night before. They set in the west a little earlier than they did the night before.

THE EASTERN SKY AT 9:00 P.M.
IN NOVEMBER

THE EASTERN SKY AT 9:00 P.M.
IN DECEMBER

These star maps show how the sky changes
through the year. These constellations will be
seen about 9:00 P.M. in the evening if you
face southward.

18

If you face south, stars rising in the
east are on your left. Constellations setting
in the west are on your right. The stars over
your head and behind you are at the top.

The imaginary red line running through the
stars is called the ECLIPTIC, the path of the
Sun. When the Sun is between us and a star
group, those stars can't be seen.

ECLIPTIC — ee-KLIP-tick

The ecliptic, or path of the Sun, passes through twelve constellations which all together are called the ZODIAC. The planets and our Moon also pass through the Zodiac.

ZODIAC — ZOH-dee-ak

Spiral Galaxy
ANDROMEDA

MILKY

W

PISCES THE FISHES

LACER
THE LIZA

GREAT SQUARE

CETUS THE WHALE

EAST

Circlet

PEGASUS
THE FLYING HORSE

ecliptic

AQUARIUS THE
WATER-BEARER

SOUTH

The foggy band of light, which is brightest
in the constellation Sagittarius, is made of
millions of faint, faraway stars. The band
is called the Milky Way.

22

SAGITTARIUS — saj-uh-TAIR-ee-us

It is easy to find the bright triangle
made by the first magnitude stars Deneb, Vega,
and Altair. Look for the square of Pegasus,
the Flying Horse, in the east.

DENEB — DEN-eb
PEGASUS — PEG-uh-suss

CAMELOPARDALIS
THE GIRAFFE

GEMINI
THE TWINS

Capella

AURIGA
THE CHARIOTEER

MONOCEROS
THE UNICORN

PERSE

MILKY   WAY

Betelgeuse

ORION

Pleiad

AST   Sirius

Aldebaran

Bellatrix

CANIS MAJOR
THE GREATER DOG

TAURUS THE BULL

Rigel

ERIDANUS THE RIVER

COLUMBA THE DOVE

LEPUS THE HARE

SOUTH

Stars seem bright in winter because the air is so clear. Look for Orion and his dogs. The Pleiades, or Seven Sisters, are a small pattern of stars, easy to find.

24

Find Capella, the "goat star" in Auriga.
Do you see the V of stars that makes the horns
of Taurus the Bull? The bright star is called
Aldebaran.

GEMINI — JEM-in-eye
ALDEBARAN — al-DEB-uh-ran

Long ago, people could only watch the stars with their eyes. In about 1608, the telescope was invented. It lets us see and photograph stars too dim to be seen with the eyes alone.

Astronomers also use the spectroscope, an instrument that helps tell how hot stars are, how fast they are moving, and even what kind of chemicals they are made of.

This very large telescope is used for taking pictures. The place where astronomers work is called an observatory.

200-INCH TELESCOPE
PALOMAR MOUNTAIN, CALIFORNIA

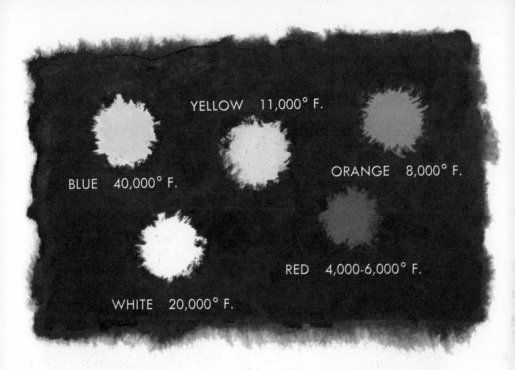

YELLOW 11,000° F.

BLUE 40,000° F.

ORANGE 8,000° F.

RED 4,000-6,000° F.

WHITE 20,000° F.

Today, astronomers know much more about the stars than people of long ago. They know that stars have different sizes. Our Sun is a "middle-sized" star. Some stars are larger than the Sun, some smaller. They glow in different colors. The coolest stars are red, like Betelgeuse. The next hottest are orange, like Aldebaran. Then come the hotter yellow stars, like our Sun, and the white stars, like Sirius. Hottest are the blue stars, like Rigel.

This cloud of glowing gas,
called the Crab Nebula, is
left over from a supernova
that exploded in 1054.

NEBULA — NEB-you-luh

Some stars are not as quiet as our Sun.
They grow larger, then smaller, then larger
again. Astronomers see them dim and brighten.
These are called VARIABLE STARS.

Other stars explode suddenly and become
thousands of times brighter all at once. They
are called NOVAS or SUPERNOVAS. Soon the
light of the exploding star fades away.

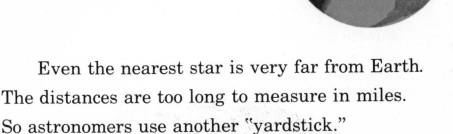

LIGHT TAKES 4⅓ YEARS TO TRAVEL TO EARTH A DISTANCE OF 25 TRILLION (25,000,000,000,000) MILES

THE EARTH

The light that we see coming from Alpha Centauri started on its way to us over four years ago. Other stars are much farther off.

Even the nearest star is very far from Earth. The distances are too long to measure in miles. So astronomers use another "yardstick."

A beam of light travels very quickly. It goes 186,000 miles a second. In one year, light travels nearly six trillion miles. That distance is called a LIGHT-YEAR. It is the astronomer's measure of distance.

Alpha Centauri, the nearest star to the Sun, is a little over four light-years from us.

All the stars we can see, and many others, make up a very large star group shaped like a wheel. It is called a GALAXY. There are over one hundred billion stars in our galaxy, and our Sun is one of them. If we look through our galaxy long-ways, all the billions of stars form a foggy band, the Milky Way.

Other galaxies can be seen by telescope. There are tens of billions of them. All the galaxies together make up the vast UNIVERSE in which we live.

Our Sun and its planets are far out toward the edge of the Milky Way Galaxy.

WORDS YOUNGER CHILDREN MAY NEED HELP WITH

(Numbers refer to page on which the word first appears.)

4	million		Betelgeuse	24	Pleiades
	traveled		Sirius	25	Castor
6	scattered	12	rotates		Pollux
	twinkle	13	Polaris		Gemini
7	constellations		compasses		Taurus
	scientists		directions		Aldebaran
	astronomers	14	horizon	26	telescopes
	pattern	15	opposite		photograph
	Ursa Major		Centaurus		spectroscope
	Ursa Minor	20	imaginary		instrument
8	Orion		ecliptic		chemicals
	shield	21	Zodiac	28	variable
9	Canis Major	22	Sagittarius		novas
	Canis Minor	23	triangle		supernovas
10	magnitude		Deneb	29	Alpha Centauri
	famous		Vega	30	galaxy
11	compared		Altair		

THINGS TO DO

Learn to find the constellations. Using the star maps on pages 18-25, learn to find the largest and brightest constellations. Tie a handkerchief over a flashlight to dim it so that your eyes will not be dazzled when you look at this book outdoors at night.

Remember that stars are brightest on cloudless nights when the Moon is not in the sky. The bright lights of the city make it hard to see any but the brightest stars.

First, locate the constellations of the northern sky: the two Bears, Cassiopeia the Queen, and Cepheus the King.

In spring, find Bootes the Herdsman rising in the east. Its bright star, Arcturus, is a sign of spring. In the south, find Leo the Lion and Gemini the Twins.

In summer, find Corona Borealis, the Northern Crown, high

overhead next to Hercules. In the south, find Scorpius the Scorpion and its red "heart," Antares.

In autumn, find the bright triangle of stars formed by the first magnitude stars Deneb, Vega, and Altair in the constellations Cygnus the Swan, Lyra the Lyre, and Aquila the Eagle. The constellation Aquarius the Water Carrier has a Y-shaped "water jar."

In winter, find Orion and his Dogs, the Pleiades next to bright Aldebaran in the constellation Taurus the Bull, and the square of Pegasus the Flying Horse toward the west.

Some stars change in brightness. Mira, in the star group Cetus the Whale, is a variable star that grows brighter and dimmer because it shrinks, then swells larger. It takes Mira a long time to change in brightness. Check it in October, when it first rises in the east, and then again in January, when it is in the west.

Algol, the Demon Star in Perseus, seems to change in brightness every three days. It is not really a swelling variable. Instead, it is a double star with a dimmer companion that goes around it and gets between Algol and us, blotting out some of Algol's light. People of long ago noticed Algol and thought it was a magic star.

See star clusters, another galaxy, and a nebula. A star cluster is a group of stars that are really close together and moving together. You need field glasses or a small telescope to see these groups well. Look for the star cluster in Hercules, Berenice's Hair between Bootes and Leo, and the Beehive in Cancer the Crab.

Another galaxy, the Great Spiral in Andromeda, looks like a tiny patch of light. It is more than two billion light-years away.

A nebula is a patch of glowing gas. You can see the Great Nebula in Orion, a patch of glowing light surrounding the stars in the hunter's sword. The nebula lies within our own galaxy.

Visit a planetarium. A planetarium has an instrument that can show the motions of the stars and planets. You sit in a dark room and the instrument shines points of light on the ceiling that look like stars. A planetarium can help us understand the motions of the stars, the Sun, the Moon, and the planets.